Volume 20! Thanks for picking it up! My little
sister's friend's son is a fan of Jiro, and I hear
he was influenced enough to start taking guitar
lessons! Jiro is one rocking girl who can play
both guitar and bass! Rock on, Kyoka Jiro!!

KOHEI HORIKOSHI

MY HERO ACADEMIA

20

SHONEN JUMP Manga Edition

STORY & ART KOHEI HORIKOSHI

TRANSLATION & ENGLISH ADAPTATION **Caleb Cook**
TOUCH-UP ART & LETTERING **John Hunt**
DESIGNER **Julian [JR] Robinson**
SHONEN JUMP SERIES EDITOR **John Bae**
GRAPHIC NOVEL EDITOR **Mike Montesa**

BOKU NO HERO ACADEMIA © 2014 by Kohei Horikoshi
All rights reserved.
First published in Japan in 2014 by SHUEISHA Inc., Tokyo.
English translation rights arranged by SHUEISHA Inc.

The stories, characters and incidents mentioned in this publication are entirely fictional.

Printed in the U.S.A.

Published by VIZ Media, LLC
P.O. Box 77010
San Francisco, CA 94107

10 9 8 7 6 5 4 3 2
First printing, August 2019
Second printing, April 2020

 VIZ MEDIA
viz.com

 SHONEN JUMP
shonenjump.com

HEAD-HAIR SHUFFLE CHARACTER
LINEUP!!

It's terrible!! Last time, the Meddler jumbled up class 1-A's brains and bodies. But this other guy named Swop T. Hairington lives across from the Meddler's parents' house, and he's causing trouble this time!!

His Quirk lets him shuffle people's hair around!! They're all having plenty of fun with their new dos!! Can you tell who's got whose style?!

Hmph.

EVIL

4 OCHACO URARAKA

3 KATSUKI BAKUGO

2 ALL MIGHT

1 IZUKU MIDORIYA

8 MOMO YAOYOROZU

7 TENYA IIDA

6 SHOTO TODOROKI

5 SHOTA AIZAWA

One day, people began manifesting special abilities that came to be known as "Quirks," and before long, the world was full of superpowered humans. But with the advent of these exceptional individuals came an increase in crime, and governments alone were unable to deal with the situation. At the same time, others emerged to oppose the spread of evil! As if straight from the comic books, these heroes keep the peace and are even officially authorized to fight crime. Our story begins when a certain Quirkless boy and lifelong hero fan meets the world's number one hero, starting him on his path to becoming the greatest hero ever!

S T O R Y

vol. 20 MY HERO ACADEMIA

CONTENTS

School Festival Start!!

SEXY.

NOT WHAT I'D EXPECT FROM SUCH A VIOLENT GAL!

HA HA HA HA HA HA HA HA HA

Ooh!!

BWA HA HA HA! WHAT'S WITH THAT GETUP, KENDO?!

NO. 178 - THE WOMAN CALLED LA BRAVA

RUSH RUSH

A COMPLIMENT, OF COURSE!! I'M THE ONE WHO ENTERED YOU INTO THIS THING IN THE FIRST PLACE!!

AND YOU BOYS HAD BETTER STOP RUSHING IN HERE.

1-B PREP ROOM

IS THAT A COMPLIMENT OR AN INSULT?

AND ONCE YOU DO, THAT'LL MAKE CLASS 1-B EVEN MORE PLUS ULTRA!

YOU'RE SURE TO WIN, SINCE THAT COMMERCIAL MADE YOU SO POPULAR!

HEY, HEY, HANG ON NOW. ARE YOU SURE SHE'LL WIN?

PEEK

WHY ARE YOU SO CONFI-DENT?

NEJIRE HADO!

BUT MORE IMPORTANTLY, I GET A REPRIEVE FROM YOUR WICKED SWINGS IN THE MEANTIME!!

HA HA HA HA HA HA

WELL... IF I'M GONNA DO IT, MIGHT AS WELL TRY TO WIN.

FWIP
FWIP

Not if you're talking about winners!!

Oh my. Don't count me out just yet!

I'M HAPPY TO BE COMPETING WITH YOU, KENDO!

BIBIMI KENRANZAKI !!

For I am the ultimate beauty here...

OHOHO OHOHO

BATTLE OF THE BABES!

Oho ho ho ho ho!

...AND CLASS B'S SHOW COMES RIGHT AFTER THAT.

CLASS A'S PERFORMANCE STARTS AT TEN...

THEN LUNCH, THEN THE BEAUTY PAGEANT.

ALMOST THERE.

YEAH ...!

WE SURE ARE EXCITED TO SEE MIDORIYA, RIGHT, ERI?

MORN- ING.

GOOD MORNING! WHAT ARE YOU UP TO?

WHAT? I'M IN PEAK CONDITION RIGHT NOW!!

HATSUME. YOU, UM, MIGHT WANT TO FIX YOURSELF UP BEFORE THE PRESENTATION.

HE HEADED DOWN THE HILL TO GO SHOPPING.

YEAH. THE BOY HAD TWO OR THREE THINGS HE HAD TO PICK UP.

PLUCK

TODAY ?!

PERMISSION TO LEAVE THE GROUNDS?

Better not turn my head.

YOUTHFUL ENTHUSIASM I GET, BUT COME ON...

WITH EVERYTHING ABOUT TO START? HE'S KINDA CUTTING IT CLOSE...

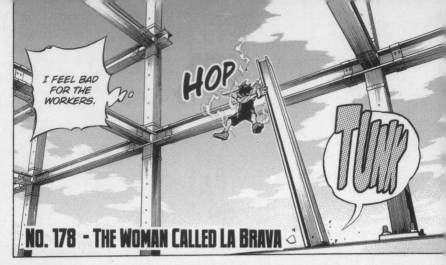

No. 178 - The Woman Called La Brava

...UNTIL OUR GRAND EXIT, YET...

BOING

I HAD HOPED TO SAVE YOUR QUIRK...

BUT, BUT!! AT THIS RATE OUR WHOLE PLAN WILL BE RUINED!

BOING

WATCH CLOSELY!

...I HAVE NO CHOICE BUT TO ASK THIS OF YOU, LA BRAVA.

AS WE'RE UNDER A TIME LIMIT...

SKF

I AM WELL AWARE!!

FWIP

BOOM

ALREADY HERE?!

DODGING MY AIR BLAST THREW OFF HIS FORM.

BOING!

BWOOOM!

...HE THREW UP ANOTHER AIR BARRIER IN ORDER TO LAND.

WHILE RIGHTING HIMSELF...

I NOTED THE EXACT SPOT...

WORMP

ON TOP OF THIS TREE!!

I CANNOT MOVE A MUSCLE ...!!

GUH

JUST GIVE UP, BOTH OF YOU!

YOU'D BETTER NOT RESIST EITHER, MISS!

I STAKE MY VERY BEARD AND SOUL ON THIS CAPER.

NORMALLY, GENTLE KNOWS IT'S TIME TO TURN TAIL WHEN WE GET SPOTTED ...!!

NOW THAT DETERMINATION'S BACKFIRING...!!

OH, GENTLE...!!

YOU KNOW AIBA, IN CLASS 3? THE TINY ONE?

I HAVEN'T EVEN SPOKEN TWO WORDS TO HER, BUT SHE SENT ME A LOVE LETTER.

FOR REAL?!

YEARBOOK

FIRST SUMMER BREAK IN MIDDLE SCHOOL...

SCARY! SOUNDS LIKE A STALKER TO ME!!

THAT GIRL WROTE OUT DOZENS OF PAGES OF THAT CRAP...

SHE WENT ON ABOUT HOW COOL I AM WHEN I DO THIS AND THAT...

PRETTY OBVIOUS SHE'S BEEN FOLLOWING ME AROUND.

GET THIS...

AFTER THAT, I DIDN'T LET MYSELF BELIEVE IN ANYONE OR ANYTHING.

I FOUND THE COURAGE TO CONFESS TO THE BOY I LIKED AND GOT MOCKED FOR IT.

GREETINGS, VIEWERS...

BUT THEN I FOUND HIM...

I EVEN THOUGHT ABOUT ENDING MY LIFE.

WITH NO AMBITIONS, I SPENT MY DAYS GLUED TO MY COMPUTER.

I FOUND YOU.

MY LIGHT.

YES, IT IS I!! GENTLE!! GENTLE CRIMINAL!!

YES!! I PLAN TO CHANGE THIS WORLD OF OURS!!

DISSATISFIED WITH THE STATE OF THINGS? I SHALL GIVE YOU SOMETHING TO BELIEVE IN!!

I SURE HOPE HE DOESN'T THINK THEY'RE GROSS.

THERE'S NOTHING I CAN DO ABOUT THESE DARK RINGS.

GENTLE CRIMINAL.

BUT YOU NEVER SAID A WORD. YOU ACCEPTED ME FOR ME.

CODE NAME LA BRAVA. WHAT DO YOU SAY?

MISS MANAMI AIBA.

Hot compress

GENTLE!! MY DEAR GENTLE!

IN MY ESTIMATION, WE MAKE THE PERFECT TEAM.

THEY'LL BE HERE SOON.

I'M HANDING YOU OVER TO THE POLICE.

QUIRK:

THANK YOU.

LA BRAVA.

I LOVE YOU.

LA BRAVA

LOVE

...I ALWAYS EDIT OUT THIS PART.

WHICH IS WHY...

ENJOY A NICE NAP, IF YOU WILL.

...THE TARGET GROWS DOZENS OF TIMES STRONGER.

SORRY ABOUT THIS, IZUKU MIDORIYA.

THE CONTRIBUTION

We made it to volume 20! I've been drawing this for four years straight! And it's all thanks to you—the readers!! In this book, we've even got congratulatory art from two other artists!!

The first one, you're probably already familiar with—Betten Court is the artist for the spin-off series in *Jump+*, *My Hero Academia: Vigilantes*!! When they first told me, "You're getting a full-blown spin-off drawn by Betten Court," I was dumbstruck. It was especially awe-inspiring and a little scary to hear, since as a kid, I regularly read *Prince Standard* and *Ashita Dorobo*. Thank you so much for getting involved with *MHA*, Betten Sensei!

The other is Yoko Akiyama, who has her own serialization in *Jump+* called *Saguri-chan Tankentai*!! She started out as an assistant helping me with *MHA*, and from the outset, it was almost frustrating just how good she was at drawing cute girls. I'd grind my teeth and stew over the quality of her drawings, seriously. Thank you for all you've done and continue to do, Akiyama Sensei!!

Volume 5 of *Vigilantes* and volume 3 of *Saguri-chan* released at the same time as this book in Japan. They both have some illustrations from me, so if you're interested, go ahead and check those out! Doing art swaps like this is so exciting! I love it!

Akiyama Sensei's art is on page 60!!

Betten Sensei's art is on page 42!

Good Moorrnin'!

NO. 179 - SCHOOL FESTIVAL START!!

HEY, GUYS!! HOPE YOU'RE READY, CUZ IT'S FINALLY TIME!!

AW, YEAH. HERE WE GO.

*U.A. AMUSEMENT PARK SIGNS: CLASS 2-D'S QUIRKY ATTRACTION

SNIFF

SNIFF

SNIFF

TODAY'S THE DAY WHEN CLASS YEAR AND DEPARTMENT DON'T MATTER—WE'RE ALL JUST HERE TO CUT LOOSE!!

NOW SAY IT WITH ME, EVERYONE.

SCHOOL FESTIVAL ...

POP

No. 179 - School Festival Start!!

···GIINN!!

HOW'D HE...?!

UNTHINKABLE, BOY!!

FL IP

PLEASE!

USING OUR LOVER MODE TO OVERCOME THE ODDS!!

A LAST RESORT, JUST LIKE ALWAYS...!!

STOP THIS, PLEASE!!

AS ALWAYS!!

THE TWO OF US!!

...WASN'T STRONG ENOUGH!!

MY LOVE...

GENTLE, I'M SO, SO, SORRY!!

...THAT YOUR FEELINGS FOR ME ARE INADEQUATE!

NOT A SINGLE SOUL HAS YET TO PROVE...

"WHO'RE YOU, AGAIN?"

"AH... UMM..."

AND THIS DREAM IS NO LONGER MINE ALONE.

...WILL GIVE A MOMENT'S THOUGHT TO THE WAY I LIVED AND BE INSPIRED.

SO THAT GOING FORWARD, SOMEONE OUT THERE...

TO CARVE MY NAME IN HISTORY, FOR FUTURE GENERATIONS!

MY DREAM WOULD BE TRIFLING INDEED IF YOUR WORDS COULD MOVE ME TO ABANDON MY COURSE!

TODAY MARKS MY FIRST STEP TOWARD TRUE INFAMY.

...I ASSUME YOU CAN COMPREHEND...

AS YOU ARE A U.A. STUDENT...

...MY PENCHANT FOR DREAMING.

SHp

BOOM

ONE WITH ENOUGH GREAT DEEDS TO LAND ME IN THE TEXTBOOKS.

GENTLE, AT 18 (HIGH SCHOOL SECOND-YEAR)

I HOPE TO BECOME A HERO.

DREAMS...

WHAT'S MORE, THIS MAKES FOUR TIMES YOU'VE FLUNKED THE PROVISIONAL LICENSE EXAM.

AT THIS POINT, I HAVE TO RECOMMEND THAT YOU DROP OUT ALTOGETHER.

YOU GOT HELD BACK A YEAR BECAUSE YOU FAILED, AND OURS ISN'T EVEN A HIGH-LEVEL SCHOOL.

YOU AREN'T LISTENING, SO I'LL TELL IT TO YOU STRAIGHT, TOBITA.

I HEAR TAKESHITA ALREADY GOT SOME OFFERS FROM AGENCIES.

FEAR NOT, MOTHER.

I WILL ENDURE, UNDAUNTED!!

35

MY QUIRK COULD HAVE CUSHIONED HIS FALL.

OH NO!!

HE'S FALLING!!

UP THERE!!

HUHH?!

BOING

SUCH WAS MY JUDGMENT CALL!

THAT'S ONE CHARGE OF OBSTRUCTING PUBLIC DUTIES...

AS IT HAPPENED, YOU PREVENTED THE HERO FROM EXECUTING THE RESCUE.

THE MAN WHO FELL WILL NEED SIX MONTHS TO MAKE A FULL RECOVERY.

*GRAFFITI: SCUM, TRASH

Expulsion Notice

I'D LONG SINCE FORGOTTEN MY DREAMS!

THE SEASON FOR EATING TSUKUSHI.

SPRING. LOVELY.

HEH HEH...

SWAY

GENTLE, AT 22 (UNDEREMPLOYED)

SPRING

*TSUKUSHI IS A WILD MOUNTAIN VEGETABLE AVAILABLE IN SPRING.

YAP

YAP

I DIDN'T HAVE THE LUXURY OF PAYING THEM A PASSING THOUGHT...

YOU REMEMBER ME, OF COURSE?!

WE WERE IN THE SAME CLASS, THOUGH I WAS HELD BACK A YEAR!

YOU'VE GONE INDEPENDENT, THEN?! HOW FANTASTIC!!

TAKESHITA?! WHY, IF IT ISN'T TAKESHITA!!

NOT JUST YET!!

SURE, HE REFLECTS PEOPLE'S ATTACKS BACK AT 'EM, BUT ALWAYS JUST TO MAKE A GETAWAY!!

WE'VE USED LOVER MODE MORE TIMES THAN I CAN COUNT!

GENTLE!

I CAN LIVE WITH THAT!!

YOU FIND ME UNPRINCIPLED? MOCK ME IF YOU MUST!!

MY GENTLE DOESN'T APPROVE OF VIOLENCE.

Congratulations on the MHA movie and volume 20!!

Better

YOU CAN WIN THIS...

...GENTLE!

No. 180 - Unbeknownst

THE STEAM FROM HER QUIRK...

NOBODY'S MOCKING YOU... GENTLE CRIMINAL!

HE'S GETTING STRONGER!

MORE KEEPS COMING OUT!

NOT ONE TO ENTANGLE OURSELVES WITH!!

HE'S MAD, THEN!

I REMEMBER NOW, GENTLE!! THAT KID'S IZUKU MIDORIYA. HE FOUGHT AT THE SPORTS FESTIVAL...

BOY!!

...HOPE TO BECOME A HERO?!

WHY DO YOU...

THIS DREAM IS NO LONGER MINE ALONE.

I LOVE YOU.

WE'RE NOT SO DIFFERENT, GENTLE!

BOP

THERE ARE PEOPLE WHO RESPECTED ME FOR IT! I GOTTA HONOR THAT!

IT WAS ONE I'D TOTALLY GIVEN UP ON! BUT I HAD PEOPLE WHO DIDN'T MOCK ME FOR IT!

IT'S WAY BIGGER THAN ME!

MY DREAM'S NOT JUST ABOUT ME!!

PLUS, THERE ARE THOSE WHO HAVE SUFFERED...

URGH!

THUD!

FL'NG

ONCE I'M IN, I'LL DEACTIVATE THEIR SECURITY SYSTEM! THEN WE'RE FREE TO INFILTRATE!

HERE'S THE PC WITH THE PROGRAM I WHIPPED UP JUST FOR TODAY! THIS SPECIAL WIRELESS CONNECTION SHOULD GET ME ACCESS TO U.A.'S NETWORK, AND THEY'LL BE NONE THE WISER.

I BELIEVE! I BELIEVE IN YOU!!

NOT A SINGLE SOUL HAS YET TO PROVE THAT YOUR FEELINGS FOR ME ARE INADEQUATE!

FWIP

POP

THE BOTTOM OF THE HILL'S NOT CLOSE ENOUGH... CAN'T CONNECT.

THERE'S NO TIME TO LOSE!

YOU'RE GOING TO WIN!

I GOTTA GET CLOSER!

SHP

LA BRAVA!! IT'S TOO RISKY TO GO ALONE!

I GOTTA PLAY MY PART IN THIS!!

RUB

RUB

ALL FOR GENTLE'S SAKE!!

SO...

...I HAVEN'T YET MEASURED UP TO THE FOES OF YOUR PAST?!

BOING

MY COMPANION WILL BE DEACTIVATING YOUR SCHOOL'S SENSORS.

I MUST END THIS, FAST!!

GDAH

SKF

NO...

OH NO...!!

GASP

SMASH!!

...I'VE FOUGHT SO FAR, GENTLE.

THIS'S BEEN THE TOUGHEST BATTLE...

HUFF

HUFF

SHP

FSSHH

SOME HEROES'RE CLOSE BY!

GENTLE!

THE LOVE-BASED POWER-UP IS A TEMPORARY ONE...

...AND IS LIMITED TO A SINGLE USE PER DAY.

PLEASE... JUST RUN.

NO... STOP IT!

GET OFFA HIM!

I HAD HOPED TO SAVE YOUR QUIRK UNTIL OUR GRAND EXIT, YET...

GO AWAY!! STOP!!

GET OFFA MY GENTLE!

SO GET OFF HIM! WHERE'S OUR BRIGHT FUTURE, HUH?!

HE DIDN'T EVEN STOP FOR HIS BELOVED TEA BREAKS WHILE PLANNING IT!

GENTLE PUT HIS HEART AND SOUL INTO THIS PLAN!

LA BRAVA...

HE'S MY EVERYTHING. YOU CAN'T STEAL HIM FROM ME!

GENTLE'S MY ONLY LIGHT IN THIS WORLD!!

BUT I KNEW FULL WELL YOU WOULD NEVER LEAVE ME BEHIND...

DIDN'T I JUST TELL YOU TO RUN AWAY?!

DON'T TAKE MY GENTLE AWAY!!

"PLEEEASE? I'M ALREADY A CRIMINAL, WHAT WITH ALL THE HACKING."

"NO, YOU MAY NOT ASSIST. THAT WOULD MAKE YOU AN ACCESSORY TO MY CRIMES."

"...I'LL BE HAPPY NO MATTER WHAT HAPPENS."

"BESIDES, AS LONG AS I'M WITH YOU, GENTLE..."

IF I CAN'T BE WITH GENTLE...

...I'LL JUST DIE!!

NO. I DARESAY SHE WOULD GO ON TO COMMIT CRIMES BEYOND ANYTHING WE'VE DONE SO FAR!

SHE WOULD NEVER BE HAPPY ESCAPING ON HER OWN.

LA
BRAVA...

I MADE
HER MY
ACCOMPL-
ICE!

I
ACCEPTED
HER HELP.

I LED
HER TO
THIS
POINT.

RUST

RUST

RUST

RUST

...FOUND
HAPPINESS!

I,
TOO....

THEY'LL
SOON
LEARN
THAT LA
BRAVA
ASSISTED
ME IN
BATTLE.

SHE'S
COMMITTED
NO REAL
SIN. YET,
SHOULD
THE HEROES
CATCH
US LIKE
THIS...!

OM

GUH

SO AT
THE
VERY
LEAST...

SHP

WE CAN PRETEND THIS BATTLE NEVER HAPPENED!

FWTP

BWOP

ESSHH ...TO LESSEN...

ALL FOR HER. FOR HER BRIGHT FUTURE.

...HER CRIME.

IF ONLY... TMP.

NOW VANISH, IZUKU MIDORIYA.

WORMP

GENTLE CRIMINAL!

TAKE PRIDE, IZUKU MIDORIYA. FOR YOU...

...PROTECTED ALL THAT WAS YOURS. THIS IS YOUR WIN.

IT SEEMS I STUMBLED OVER A PEBBLE BY THE ROADSIDE.

SKWEEZ

U.A....

I SURRENDER.

CONGRATULATIONS ON VOLUME 20!!

AND THE MOVIE, AND FOUR YEARS OF SERIALIZATION!!

Congratulations on making it to 20 volumes, Horikoshi!

It feels like you went from a reprinting of volume 1 to an anime adaptation and megapopularity in the blink of an eye, and that Plus Ultra achievement makes me as happy as if it were my own!

As a devoted reader, I can't wait to see how the plot unfolds from here on out!

YOKO AKIYAMA
あきやま陽光

HEY, YOU HUNGRY, ECTOPLASM? COME TO OUR STALL!

YAP YAP

UNDERSTOOD. I'LL LOOK INTO IT.

YAP

EARLIER...

A STUDENT WHO WENT SHOPPING HASN'T RETURNED?

I'D LIKE SOME, YES...

IS THERE AN EMERGENCY?

WE NEED FOUR OR FIVE OF YOUR CLONES TO HEAD TO E-4, GRRRR.

THIS IS... GRRRR DOG, IN SECTOR C-16!

NO. 181 - FOR SOMEONE ELSE

...AND AREN'T MOVING AROUND MUCH, STAYING IN ONE SPOT.

THEY'RE OFF THE WALKING PATH...

RUSTL

I'LL LET YOU KNOW... SMELLS LIKE...THREE INDIVIDUALS...

RUSTL

I SMELL A LOT OF SWEAT, SO THEY MUST BE AGITATED.

WE'RE ON HIGH ALERT, EVERYONE...

LOST KIDS?

INJURED?

OR JUST IDIOTS?

HE'S ALSO KNOWN FOR UPLOADING MISCHIEVOUS VIDEOS.

HE'S A VILLAIN WHO SPECIALIZES IN QUICK ESCAPES.

I RECOGNIZE HIM.

SURRENDER?

AS I SAID, I TRIPPED AND FELL...!

WHAT'S WITH THE WOUNDS, HUH? AND THE TORN-UP FIELD?

NO ONE.

GENTLE!

WHO'RE YOU WORKING WITH?

SH P

COR- RECT.

JUST YOU TWO, THEN?

IT SMELLS LIKE ONE OF OUR STUDENTS!

SNIFF

CORRECT?! WHERE'S THE THIRD?

NOW VANISH, IZUKU MIDORIYA.

FOR HER BRIGHT FUTURE.

ALL FOR HER.

...WHAT GENTLE CRIMINAL WAS DOING.

IT WAS THEN THAT I SOMEHOW UNDERSTOOD...

...JUST... OVER THERE...

HE SHOULD BE...

...UNTIL ALL THAT WAS LEFT IN ME, DEEP DOWN...

I FOUGHT WITH MY FEELINGS ON THE LINE...

SO, I'M OVERJOYED THAT THIS WAS FOR YOU, IN THE END.

YET, ALL ALONG...

...I WAS DOING IT FOR ME.

I PUT A TASTEFUL SPIN ON MY SELFISH ACTIONS.

I'VE COMMITTED COUNTLESS CRIMES, BUT MY GREATEST SIN OF ALL WAS...

I AM UTTERLY STRIPPED OF THE WILL TO FIGHT BACK.

64

...THAT BEAT FOR SOME- ONE ELSE!

...ABDUCTING THIS POOR, NAIVE WOMAN...

...WAS A HEART...

...AND BRAIN- WASHING HER.

...TO PARDON MANAMI AIBA!

SO I ASK YOU NOW...

GENTLE ...!!

IT'S NOT RIGHT!

YOU'RE DOING THIS FOR ME?!

...WAS AGAINST YOU.

I'M GLAD THAT MY FINAL, CLIMACTIC CLASH...

YOUR INJURIES!

IZUKU MIDORIYA.

YOU
KNOW
THAT!

I NEVER
WANTED
TO MAKE
TROUBLE
FOR YOU,
GENTLE.

IT'S
NOT
FAIR!

I LOVE YOU
WITH ALL
MY HEART,
GENTLE.

YOU
FOUGHT
THIS
GUY?

I FIGURED OUT THAT HE WAS GOING TO PRANK U.A.

SO YEAH... WE FOUGHT A LITTLE.

EVERY-THING'S OKAY NOW.

BUT...

AHHHH!

WAHHH!

SNIPE?

COME IN, HOUND DOG! ECTOPLASM C! RUSTLE UP ANYTHING STRANGE?

...

WE'RE WAITING FOR A REPORT, HERE.

KEEP EVERYONE ON ALERT, THOUGH.

CAN'T SAY I GET IT EITHER, BUT...

THE HECK?

JUST SOME TROUBLEMAKER WHO UPLOADS PRANK VIDEOS. HE WANTS TO TURN HIMSELF IN.

TNG

...THERE'S NO EMERGENCY, FOR NOW.

IZUKU MIDORIYA...

YOU'LL EXPLAIN YOURSELF IN DETAIL OVER AT THE POLICE STATION.

GENTLE CRIMINAL IS A MERE SHADOW OF A FAILED WOULD-BE HERO.

I, TOO, WAS ONCE ENROLLED IN A HERO COURSE.

THOUGH I AM IN NO POSITION TO GIVE ADVICE...

YOU'D STEAL A SMILE FROM A GIRL WHO DOESN'T KNOW THE MEANING OF JOY YET?!

THOSE FEELINGS OF YOURS—MAKE SURE TO SEE THEM THROUGH.

A BRIGHT FUTURE...?

HOW DID I END UP SO UTTERLY DISSATISFIED?

BECAUSE I WAS FECKLESS AND COWARDLY.

CLASS A'S PERFORMANCE STARTS AT TEN, RIGHT? IT'S 9:16 NOW... NO, 9:17.

AH!

ALL MIGHT WAS WORRIED ABOUT YOU.

GENTLE CRIMINAL...

WHERE? I'LL COME WITH YOU.

I'M SO SORRY, SENSEI, BUT I LEFT MY SHOPPING BAGS BACK THERE!

STILL...WE'LL BE BACK AT SCHOOL IN FIVE OR SIX MINUTES.

...WAS A TOUGH OPPONENT.

YEESH!

BROOO

WHY'S IT TAKING HIM THIS LONG TO DO A LITTLE SHOPPING?

HUH? WHERE'S MIDORIYA?

BAND 9:25 A.M.

I UNDERSTOOD WHY FIGHTING HIM WAS SO HARD FOR ME.

"A MERE SHADOW OF A FAILED WOULD-BE HERO."

IT WAS BECAUSE I MIGHT'VE TURNED OUT THAT WAY, TOO.

GENTLE AND I HAD SIMILAR FEELINGS.

WHILE I...

HIS FEELINGS CONCERNED LA BRAVA.

9:35 A.M.

HMPH!

KINDA PUMPED TO SEE IT.

WONDER HOW CLASS 1-A'S THING IS GONNA TURN OUT?

DEKU'S NOT GONNA DANCE?

THEY'VE BEEN EXCITED SINCE THIS MORNING.

THE MORONS'RE JUST LOOKING FORWARD TO WHAT WE'VE GOT FOR 'EM!

THERE'RE WAY MORE PEOPLE THAN I EXPECTED.

I SHOULD SAY SO...

A FINE TIME HE PICKED TO BLOW US OFF!!!

WHERE'S DEKU, AOYAMA?!

9:59 A.M.

OH!

OHH!

OH!

IT'S STARTING!

C'MON, FIRST-YEARS!!

YAOYOROZU!!

HERE WE GO!

CLAP

WOOOO

CLAP

CLAP

YEAHHH

YAOYOROZU!! YAOYOROZU!!

YAOYO-ROZU!

WHAT'D THESE FIRST-YEARS COOK UP?!

CLAP

CLAP

SHAH

LET'S DO THIS, DAMMIT!!

WHILE I...

YEAH...!

LOOK, ERI!

SEE HIM?!

...JUST WANTED TO SEE YOU SMILE!

SUPER-DUPER WONDER COSTUMES WITH INCREASING/DECREASING BUTTON COUNTS

NO. 182 - LET IT FLOW! SCHOOL FESTIVAL!

GO CLEAN YOURSELF UP. THERE'S STILL TIME.

HOW WILL ANYONE ENJOY THE SHOW WHEN THEY'RE WORRIED ABOUT YOU?

GET BACK TO YOUR POST.

NOBODY ASKED YOU.

DOUBTS?! OVER WHAT?! I'M HYPED!

I...DON'T KNOW ABOUT THIS.

I JUST WANT A QUICK LOOKSEE!

SHIRKING PATROL DUTIES

CHAPERONING ERI

AND SOME BLAME THEIR FRUSTRATIONS ON CLASS 1-A.

THERE ARE MANY STUDENTS IN THE AUDIENCE IN OTHER DEPARTMENTS AND GRADES WHO AREN'T HAPPY WITH U.A.

THOSE MALCONTENTS AREN'T HERE TO HAVE FUN. THEY'RE HERE TO CRITICIZE THE PERFORMANCE.

I THINK IT'S FAIR TO SAY THEY'RE NOT HERE FOR THE ENTERTAINMENT.

BUT IT SEEMS LIKE THEY'RE JUST DOING IT FOR THEMSELVES.

A BAND? A DANCE SQUAD?

SURE... I BET THEY'LL PERFORM WELL.

LET'S DO THIS, DAMMIT!

WE'LL GRAB HOLD OF U.A. ...

KYOKA.

YOU SHOULD DO WHAT YOU WANT.

"...SO I WAS THINKING THIS MIGHT BE JUST THE THING TO CHEER HER UP!"

"SHE'S BEEN THROUGH SO MUCH..."

A SURPRISE? ERI'S GOING TO BE AT THE FESTIVAL?

...TO SHINE!

NOW IT'S TIME FOR AOYAMA AND MIDORIYA...

THEY'RE IN PERFECT SYNC...

MIDORIYA AND LASER BOY!

HERE IT COMES !!

Oui! ☆

READY ?!

A HUMAN
FIRECRACKER!

ALMOST
TIME.

GRITTIER

OOZE

CATCH!

Dof!

Oui!

SORRY
...

I'M NOT GONNA BE A MUSICIAN...

IT'S JUST THAT PUTTING MYSELF ON THE LINE TO FIGHT FOR OTHERS IS SO COOL!

YOU DON'T GET IT! I'VE BEEN STRUGGLING WITH THIS ALL ALONG!

RUB RUB

HEY! WHAT'S THERE TO CRY ABOUT?

AT FIRST, IT WAS JUST COOL AND FUN AND WE WERE GOOD AT IT.

BASIC STUFF LIKE THAT.

YOU SHOULD DO WHAT YOU WANT.

KYOKA.

YOUR MOM AND I WENT WITH MUSIC CUZ THAT'S WHAT WE LOVED.

I'VE ALWAYS ADMIRED WHAT YOU DO, MOM AND DAD... BUT NOW THE MUSIC YOU TAUGHT ME IS GONNA GO TO WASTE.

OUR FAMILY'S SO PASSIONATE ABOUT MUSIC... WHICH'S WHY I COULDN'T TELL YOU.

BUT THE LONGER WE PURSUED IT, THE MORE WE REALIZED...

IN THAT SENSE...

...THE MUSIC WE MADE COULD ACTUALLY DO SOMETHING FOR OTHERS...

...MUSIC AND HEROISM AREN'T SO DIFFERENT.

HYPOCRITE!

BAM

BAM

OF COURSE IT'S ALL GONNA FALL APART WHEN YOU START SHOWBOATING!

STOP SPEEDING UP THE TEMPO, DUMMY!

HUH?

NO WEIRD AD-LIBBING TOMORROW, OKAY?

MIDORIYA!!

SIR NIGHTEYE!!

ARE YOU TWO WATCHING?

AH! MIDORIYA!!

SIR!!

94

JUMP MAG VS. GRAPHIC NOVEL EDITION

Chapter 182.

This chapter was rough and sketchy when it came out in *Shonen Jump*, and I felt terrible about it. Especially for the readers who follow the story via the weekly chapters. Of all the chapters for this to happen… You couldn't even tell what was going on in some spots. It's all fixed up for this book, of course, and I've even added some additional bits and shifted things around to better fit my original vision.

Jiro's close-up gets a two-page spread, for one.

That's how I originally wanted to do it, so please think of this as an apology.

Still, I liked the version of Jiro I drew for the chapter in the magazine, so it's included below.

"You should do what you want." Thank you, Kyotoku (Jiro's dad).

NOW HEAR ME, COUNT PARIS, PHANTOM OF AZKABAN! I SHALL BE TAKING BACK MY JULIET!!

MY NAME IS ROMEO!!

NO. 183 - FESTIVAL ALL DAY LONG!!

BUT, ROMEO... WHAT OBI-WAN TOLD YOU ABOUT YOUR FATHER...

THAT HE WAS THE KING OF GONDOR... THAT WAS A LIE.

I AM YOUR FATHER!

NOOOOO!!

BAM

YAP YAP

IT WAS KINDA FUNNY HOW THEY WERE SO INTO IT.

THAT WAS NUTS!

TALK ABOUT THE ULTIMATE CROSSOVER EVENT!!

THAT'S JUST HOW IT IS... WE GOTTA CLEAN UP THE MESS WE MADE!

YAP

YAP

WISH WE COULD'VE SEEN CLASS B'S PLAY.

I RAN OUT WITHOUT IT...

BUT AT LEAST PICK UP YOUR PHONE.

BEING LATE WASN'T THE ISSUE.

SOMEBODY'S IN TROUBLE!

YOU'LL BE SHOCKED.

CHECK YOUR MISSED CALLS...

GOOD JOB BACK THERE.

I GOT THE GIST OF IT FROM ECTO.

I'M SORRY FOR MAKING EVERYONE WORRY.

SHOOT

DON'T GO THINKING WHAT YOU DID WAS RIGHT!

YOU'RE STILL A STUDENT HERE, WITH ONLY A PROVISIONAL LICENSE!

BUT THAT DOESN'T MAKE IT OKAY!

PANT

THE SHOW DIDN'T GET CANCELED BECAUSE YOU WEREN'T HURT TOO BAD!

PANT PANT

WE'RE HERE TO PROTECT YOU KIDS!

WHEN THERE'S A FIGHT, YOU RELY ON US!

HNF!

WHAM

THE FESTIVAL'S STILL ON, SO HAVE FUN, DAMMIT!!

RIGHT.

WIPE THAT GLOOMY LOOK OFF YOUR MUG AND GET GOING.

?!

THANK YOU, HOUND DOG.

PANT PANT

OH. YOU'RE HERE, DEKU.

LOOK, ERI! MIDORIYA CAME FLYING AT US!

THUD

YOU ONLY FORGET HOW TO TALK WHEN YOU'RE BARKING MAD...

WOOFWOOF

ROWF! GRRRR...

THRASH

YOU'RE RIGHT. I WAS CARELESS...

HOWWWWL MIGHT!!

HEYYY, NICE SHOW!

From now on, you're known as "Errand Boy"...

...EVERYONE WAS DANCING AND JUMPING AROUND!

AT FIRST, THE BIG NOISES WERE SCARY, BUT THEN...

THAT ONE GIRL'S SINGING WAS REALLY INTENSE, AND...

AND IT GOT ALL COLD, LIKE "WHOOSH"!

AND THE LIGHTS WERE SPINNING EVERY-WHERE!

THEN THERE WAS A FLASHY LIGHT AND YOU DISAPPEARED, DEKU!

IT WAS AMAZING!

I'M SO GLAD YOU LIKED IT.

RUB RUB

Carry these as well! ☆

AHH! SORRY, I'M HELPING! I'M HELPING!

YEAH? WELL, I WON'T BE GLAD IF WE'RE LATE! HELP OUT, SLACKER!

WOW! THANKS A LOT!!

THAT WAS SICK! AND CRAZY FUN!

YO, CLASS A!!

IT'S GREAT THAT IT WAS SO FUN.

YEAH...

...

YAP YAP

WE WERE JUST HOPING YOU'D FAIL!!

SORRY, OKAY?!

INDEED!

THAT MEANS YOUR PLAN WORKED LIKE A CHARM, IDA!!

THEY MUST'VE BEEN STRESSED OUT, JUST LIKE SENSEI MENTIONED.

FLAWLESS VICTORY!

THEY REALLY DIDN'T HAVE TO TELL US THAT...

SCAMPER

WE GOT THE MESSAGE, LOUD AND CLEAR.

WE HEARD WHAT YOU WERE TRYING TO ACCOMPLISH WITH ALL THIS.

DON'T SWEAT IT.

IF ONLY WE COULD DO SOMETHING FOR THOSE WHO COULDN'T BE IN OUR AUDIENCE...

HOWEVER! WE ONLY GOT THROUGH TO THEM BECAUSE THEY CAME TO WATCH.

THIS'LL BE OUR WAY OF PAYING YOUR MESSAGE FORWARD.

WE'LL DO OUR BEST TO HELP OTHERS HAVE A GOOD TIME, TOO.

WHOA... HA HA HA!

HA HA HA!

JUST CUT IT OUT! SERIOUSLY...

THAT AIN'T SATISFYING... LET'S FIND WHOEVER DIDN'T WATCH AND DRAG 'EM OUT HERE!

THANK YOU FOR YOUR SUPPORT!

PRETTY GREAT, HUH?

...WE WON'T GET SEATS AT THE BEAUTY PAGEANT!

IF WE DON'T HURRY...

OKAY, OKAY, SORRY! WHAT'S EATING YOU, MINETA?

GET BACK TO WORK!! WE GOTTA FINISH CLEANING UP THIS DUMB ICE!!

YEA

H

H

KRAK

KRAK

HAHH
!!

KENDO
!!

WITH HER LOVELY DRESS, TORN TO SHREDS BY A MARTIAL ARTS DEMO, HER FANTASTIC PERFORMANCE COMBINES STRENGTH AND BEAUTY!!

WHAT A BREATH OF FRESH AIR!!

RRMM

BBB

HOW DULL!! THIS GIRL UNDERSTANDS NOTHING, AND SHE'LL NEVER MEASURE UP TO ME!!

FROM THE THIRD-YEAR SUPPORT COURSE, IT'S THE PAGEANT QUEEN HERSELF!

SHE'S COMBINING HER TECHNICAL SKILLS WITH HER OWN BEAUTIFUL FACE, MAKING FOR A STUNNING PERFORMANCE!

MY SPLEN-DIFEROUS GORGEOUS-NESS IS THE PINNACLE OF BEAUTY!

CONGRATS TO YOU GUYS, TOO!

HEY, I HEARD YOUR PLAY WENT OVER GREAT!

HO HO! WELL DONE, THIRD-YEAR...

I WAS FOLLOWING A SECOND AGO, BUT NOW I'M LOST!

WHAT'S THIS SHOW ABOUT AGAIN?

C'MON, HADO... JUST REMEMBER, THE PEOPLE IN THE AUDIENCE ARE NOTHING BUT MAMMALS. YOU'LL BE FINE.

NEJIRE...

THANKS FOR COMING TODAY! WE HAD FUN, RIGHT?!

ERI, LOOK...

YEAH...

SURPRISE!

FWIP

TMP TMP TMP

IT DIDN'T LOOK LIKE THERE'D BE ANY, BASED ON THE PROGRAM, SO...

THE CONVENIENCE STORE DIDN'T HAVE RED FOOD DYE, BUT SATO LENT ME SOME.

I PICKED UP THE INGREDIENTS WHEN I WENT SHOPPING. THEY'RE EASIER TO MAKE THAN I THOUGHT!

APPLES!

I BET THEY'LL HAVE CANDIED APPLES!

SOMEONE WAS SELLING THEM?! I LOOKED EVERY-WHERE!!

A CANDY APPLE!

Here, take one.

EXTRA SWEET!

HEH...

YOU'LL BE ABLE TO SEE THEM AGAIN SOON, I EXPECT.

NIP

I CAN ALWAYS MAKE MORE, SO LOOK FORWARD TO IT.

THROB

FLIK FLIK

YES.

INCREDIBLE!

YOU TAUGHT YOURSELF TO DO ALL THIS?

WHIP SH

AND YOU NEVER WANTED TO USE YOUR TALENTS TO DO GOOD IN THE WORLD?

I'M LA BRAVA.

WHAT DO YOU DO FOR A LIVING?

NEVER.

ALL I EVER WANTED WAS TO HELP GENTLE.

SHE'S ACTUALLY JUST SMITTEN WITH YOU, YEAH?

SO THAT IDIOTIC LIE WON'T FLY HERE.

THERE'S A SIMPLE TEST TO TELL IF SHE'S REALLY BRAINWASHED OR NOT.

SO YOU LOVE HER TOO? YEESH...

HMPH...

AIBA NEVER TOOK PART DIRECTLY. MY CAPITAL OFFENSES ARE NOT HERS...

SURE, PLENTY OF YOUR CRIMES WERE ONLY ATTEMPTED CRIMES, BUT THE SHEER NUMBER TELLS US SHE WAS IN ON IT.

I RECALLED THE DREAM I ONCE HELD.

IT FRIGHTENED ME, AND I DASHED FORTH, HEADLONG.

FORMERLY IN A HERO COURSE... BUT YOU WENT ASTRAY AND STARTED COMMITTING CRIMES ON VIDEO.

HIGH SCHOOL DROPOUT, HUH?

WELL, GOOD THING YOU GAVE IT ALL UP TODAY.

DOWN THE WRONG PATH, PERHAPS...

THEY'RE TOO IMPATIENT. THEY WANT RESULTS RIGHT AWAY.

...ARE THE ONES WITH NO REAL DESIRE TO CHANGE.

THE ONLY PEOPLE WHO SAY THEY CAN'T TURN THEIR LIVES AROUND...

WE ONLY GOT PLAIN OLD TEA...

FINE BLACK TEA, IF YOU WOULD...

ANYWAY, WANT SOME TEA?

THE UNIFORM

Birthday: 9/10
Height: 160 cm
Favorite Things: Everything cute

THE SUPPLEMENT
Nejire's good pal, who thinks Nejire is the cutest thing in the galaxy. Useless info: she dyes her hair, has piercings and generally does stylish stuff that wouldn't be allowed in real life.

AS NOVEMBER ENTERED ITS FINAL DAYS...

DING DONG

DING DONG

WHOSH

NO. 184 - JAPANESE HERO BILLBOARD CHART

U.A. IS TAKING HER IN.

YOU WEREN'T KIDDING ABOUT HANGING OUT AGAIN SOON!!

WELL, IT'S NOT LIKE SHE CAN STAY IN THE HOSPITAL FOREVER.

SHE REMINDS ME OF MY LITTLE SISTER.

HI, EVERY-BODY.

WOO-HOO, WE GOT OURSELVES AN ERI.

HOW'D THIS WORK OUT, EXACTLY?!

IN OTHER WORDS, SHE'S GOT NOWHERE TO CALL HOME.

SHE STILL HAS A GRANDFATHER, THE HASSAIKAI BOSS, BUT HE'S IN A COMA FOR THE FORESEEABLE FUTURE.

THEY SAY HER MOTHER ABANDONED HER.

FWIP FWIP

BUT IT'S STARTING TO GROW OUT, LITTLE BY LITTLE.

HER *HORN* IS THE SOURCE OF HER QUIRK.

PLUS, AIZAWA SENSEI MIGHT'VE MENTIONED THIS...

AND EVERYTHING SHOULD BE FINE WHILE IT'S ALL SHRUNKEN. WE HEARD...

Right.

ALL THE MORE REASON TO HAVE HER HERE WITH US INSTEAD OF AT AN ORPHANAGE.

NOD

HOLD ON... HOW DO WE KNOW *THAT* WON'T HAPPEN AGAIN?

SHE'LL BE STAYING IN THE FACULTY DORM, WHERE I'LL KEEP AN EYE ON HER.

WE'LL OBSERVE HER AND TRY TO FIGURE OUT A WAY TO DEAL WITH HER INCREDIBLE POWER.

THERE'LL ALSO BE REGULAR EXAMINATIONS... EVERYTHING... ONE STEP AT A TIME.

THAT'S WHERE I COME IN, SINCE I'M TAKING TIME OFF FROM SCHOOL! PLUS, ERI AND I ARE ALREADY PALS!

KERSHWING

THAT'S A BIG RESPONSI-BILITY, AIZAWA SENSEI.

PAT

AND ONCE ERI'S BODY AND MIND HAVE STABILIZED...

OF COURSE!

I KNOW YOU ALL HAVE BUSY LIVES, BUT STOP BY EVERY ONCE IN A WHILE.

I ADMIT, THAT WOULD BE NICE!

HA HA HA!

IT WON'T BE LONG UNTIL OUR INVINCIBLE DUDE MAKES A COMEBACK.

YOU'RE EXPECTING GUESTS.

NO. BACK TO THE DORMS, WITH THE REST OF CLASS A.

CAN WE PLAY TOO?

ROGER THAT. WE'LL PLAY OTHELLO OR SOMETHING!

IT'S SHORT NOTICE, BUT COULD YOU THIRD-YEARS WATCH HER FOR A BIT?

JOLT

ACHOO!

1-A

LIKE WHOEVER WAS SHOUTING "YAOYOROZU!"

OR MAYBE YOU HAVE SOME FANS WHO'RE GOSSIPING ABOUT YOU?!

NO... I'M IN PERFECT HEALTH, AND MY MUCUS MEMBRANES ARE FUNCTIONING PROPERLY.

ARE YOU FEELING SICK?

UH...

PLEASE DON'T TEASE ME. I'M JUST HAPPY TO HAVE AN ADMIRER!

YOU PROBABLY ALREADY HAVE A TON OF FANS, TOKOYAMI.

ESPECIALLY AFTER DOING YOUR WORK STUDY WITH HAWKS.

THEY'RE HERE, EVERYONE! LET'S GREET THEM!!

AH!!

KLIK

THAT ALL WENT A BIT *TOO QUICKLY.*

NO, I DON'T THINK SO.

I HOPE MY LITTLE KITTIES HAVE ALL BEEN WELL!

YAYYYY

PUSSYCATS! IT'S GREAT TO SEE YOU AFTER ALL THIS TIME!

PAW PAD MANJU!

PAW PAD MANJU!

WE'RE DOING GOOD, THANKS.

DON'T REMIND ME...

LOOM

SORRY WE COULDN'T PROTECT YOU, BACK THEN.

SURE...

UH-HUH.

THANKS FOR THAT LETTER! IT MEANT A LOT, REALLY!

KOTA!! LONG TIME NO SEE!!

BAM

HUH?

C-CUT IT OUT.

LOOK HERE, MIDORIYA.

NOW WE MATCH!

HE PICKED THEM HIMSELF. "THEY HAVE TO BE RED," HE SAID.

SO WHY ARE YOU HERE AT U.A.?

YOU'VE... GOT IT WRONG...

WE'RE JUST HERE TO ANNOUNCE THAT WE'RE BACK.

We've gotta go see class B anyway.

Oh, don't trouble yourselves.

FWIP FWIP

Please, have a seat.

JUST CALL ME THE *CAT*-MINISTRATIVE ASSISTANT!

NOT BACK *IN ACTION* PER SE, BUT I'LL BE IN THE AGENCY, SUPPORTING THE OTHER THREE!

SHWIP SHWIP

CONGRAT-ULATIONS!!

YOU'RE BACK?!

WITH YOUR QUIRK STOLEN, I THOUGHT YOU HAD TO QUIT?

YOU TOO, RAG-DOLL?

DEFINITELY A BAD HABIT OF MINE.

WHEN I SEE A GOOD QUIRK, I JUST NEED TO HAVE IT.

IT'S NOT RIGHT, I KNOW.

WE DID HEAR FROM HIM, IN TARTARUS...

I'D LOVE TO RETURN HERS, BUT THAT WOULD INVOLVE USING MY OWN QUIRK.

SHOULD I? JUST SAY THE WORD...

THEN WHY RETURN NOW?

SO IN THE MEANTIME, KEEPING HIM COMPLETELY IMMOBILIZED IS THE SAFEST OPTION.

THEY'RE STILL PRESSING HIM TO FIND OUT WHAT KINDS OF QUIRKS HE'S GOT LOCKED UP INSIDE HIM, AND HOW MANY.

WHY DO YOU THINK WE'RE STILL IN THE TRIPLE DIGITS, DESPITE ZERO ACTION?!

WRONG, MEOW!

OH! SO YOU'RE DOING THIS TO STOP YOUR SHARP DECLINE!!

BUT YOUR TEAM WAS 32ND LAST TIME!

BAM

WHICH MEANS PEOPLE ARE COUNTING ON US...

...SO WE CAN'T STOP MOVING FORWARD!!

OUR APPROVAL RATING, AT LEAST, WAS AS HIGH AS EVER.

NOT WITH ALL THAT'S BEEN HAPPENING.

OH YEAH. THEY HAVEN'T ANNOUNCED THIS YEAR'S SECOND RANKINGS YET.

THE BILLBOARD CHART, RIGHT...

I HEAR YOU! THE WILD, WILD PUSSYCATS ARE DUDES AMONG DUDES!!

Pipe down.

SNIFFLE

125

A BILLBOARD CHART WITHOUT ALL MIGHT, HUH?

IT'S THE FIRST BILLBOARD CHART SINCE THE KAMINO INCIDENT!!

AND EVERYONE EVERYWHERE UNDERSTANDS HOW MAJOR THIS IS!!

BILL BOARD CHARTS

CAN'T WAIT TO FIND OUT. SHOULD BE EXCITING!

THE TIMES, HOWEVER, ARE A-CHANGING! STAY TUNED!!

NEVER BEFORE HAVE HEROES TAKEN THE STAGE IN PERSON AT THIS PRESENTATION.

JUST BEING ON THE SAME TEAM AS HIM IS SO INSPIRING.

IS IT TRUE THAT YOU TWO ARE ALSO A GREAT TEAM OUTSIDE OF WORK?!

NO COMMENT.

MT. LADY: 23RD PLACE

WAHHH! WHY'S HE GET ALL THE GLORY?!

YOU'RE SPECIAL IN YOUR OWN WAY.

ROCK STEADY AS EVER, THIS ORTHODOX HERO HAS MAINTAINED HIS RANK!

NO. 6!

SHIELD HERO: CRUST!

OH, ALL MIGHT...

IT'S A GREAT LEAP FORWARD FOR THIS UP-AND-COMER!!

NO. 7!

WHAT AN HONOR.

KAMUI WOODS!

NO. 4!

THE MYSTERIOUS SHINOBI WHOSE INCIDENT RESOLUTION RATE AND SUPPORT ARE SKYROCKETING...

NINJA HERO: EDGE-SHOT!

KEEP QUIET. WE'RE IN PUBLIC.

NO. 5!

THIS UNYIELDING BUNNY WAS BUMPED UP IN THE RANKINGS!

ONLY WEAKLINGS JOIN TEAMS!

RABBIT HERO: MIRKO!

WITH A HIGHER PUBLIC SUPPORT RATE THAN ANYONE, IT'S THE FIBER HERO!

STILL AT NO. 3, EVEN THOUGH HE'S TAKING TIME OFF!

WHICH BRINGS US TO THE NEXT MAN!!

IT SEEMS ANY HERO INVOLVED WITH WHAT HAPPENED IN KAMINO HAS SEEN HIS OR HER FORTUNES RISE!

WHAT ARE YOU?!

WASHA!!

This guy is
absurdly
popular with
little kids.
I like him.

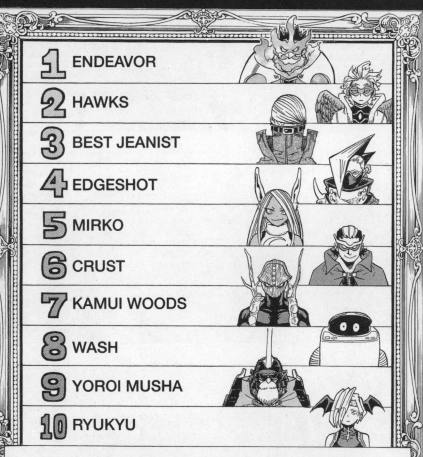

1 ENDEAVOR

2 HAWKS

3 BEST JEANIST

4 EDGESHOT

5 MIRKO

6 CRUST

7 KAMUI WOODS

8 WASH

9 YOROI MUSHA

10 RYUKYU

The Heroes Public Safety Commission looks over the past year of heroism and—after using a proprietary formula to quantify incident resolution rate, societal contributions and public approval rating—presents the results in the form of rankings.

Because incident resolution rate is the most important factor and heroes who tackle bigger incidents end up with even more public support, those involved in major crises quickly find themselves climbing the ranks.

...BECAUSE THIS IS A CRITICAL JUNCTURE FOR OUR TIMES.

WE DECIDED TO PUT ON SUCH AN ELABORATE CEREMONY...

PRESIDENT OF THE HEROES PUBLIC SAFETY COMMISSION

DUNNN

IT'S BEEN ABOUT THREE MONTHS SINCE ALL MIGHT'S RETIREMENT.

AND WORD ON THE STREET IS THAT OUR SOCIETY IS STILL MISSING AN ICON...

GLARE

BUT THE HEROES STANDING BEFORE YOU ARE READY TO TAKE ON THE MANTLE.

SO LET US JOIN THEM IN THEIR QUEST FOR A PEACEFUL SOCIETY.

PSST

HOW'S IT FEEL TO BE ON TOP?

HOW-EVER...

IN TRUTH, I WOULD'VE WITHDRAWN MY NAME IF THAT WERE ALLOWED.

THANK YOU FOR THIS HONOR.

AND NOW, A WORD FROM OUR HEROES!

...

RYUKYU!

...SO GOING FORWARD, I'LL STRIVE TO REALLY EARN MY RANKING.

THERE HAVE BEEN LIVES I COULDN'T SAVE...

WAIT YOUR TURN, CRUST...

WE CAN DO IT, RYUKYU!! I BELIEVE IN US!!

THAT'S NOT A BAD THING, I GUESS...

HE'S A LITTLE INTENSE.

THAT PAIN IN YOUR HEART! LIKE YOU'RE JUST NOT GOOD ENOUGH!!

WE NEED TO STAND TALL AND FIGHT ON!!

I FEEL YOU, RYUKYU!

WASHA!!

THE MISSION IS THE SAME AS EVER.

...SO I'D LIKE TO MAKE HIM AND ALL MY SUPERIORS PROUD.

EDGESHOT WAS KIND ENOUGH TO LET ME JOIN HIS TEAM...

...

IT STILL HURTS DEEP DOWN EVERY TIME I THINK ABOUT IT!!

ARGHHHH

WHY WASN'T I IN KAMINO THAT DAY?!

HOPE YOU'RE READY FOR ME TO KICK YOUR BUTTS.

TO ALL THE PLOTTERS AND SCHEMERS OUT THERE!!

NUMBERS DON'T CONCERN ME.

IF PUBLIC APPROVAL WERE THE ONLY FACTOR, YOU'D BE IN THIRD PLACE!

...BUT I DON'T DO THIS JOB FOR FAME OR REPUTATION.

I'M GRATEFUL TO ALL MY SUPPORTERS, OF COURSE...

THE ABILITY TO PRESERVE LAW AND ORDER IS THE TRUE MEASURE OF A HERO.

WHO THE HECK DO YOU THINK WANTS TO HEAR THAT CRAP?!

People like Stain, yeah?

Ahh!

SHP

I JUST HATE HOLDING BACK HOW I FEEL.

YOU ALWAYS DID ENJOY ROCKING THE BOAT.

SASSY. I LIKE IT!

I'D BE SECOND, EDGESHOT'D BE THIRD...

AHEM...

F

W
R
A
P

ENDEAVOR, FOURTH, AND SO ON.

BEST JEANIST WOULD BE NUMBER ONE IF THAT WAS ALL THAT MATTERED, THANKS TO THE BOOST HE'S GOTTEN DURING HIS LEAVE OF ABSENCE.

YOU WANNA TALK PUBLIC SUPPORT?

SURE... IT MATTERS MORE THAN ANYTHING ELSE NOW, BUT C'MON...

PUBLIC APPROVAL?

OUR SYMBOL'S GONE.

AND YOU SAY THAT STAYING THE COURSE IS THE ANSWER?

THIS ISN'T THE TIME TO DWELL ON THE PAST.

FWAP

FWAP

FWAP

TODAY'S A TURNING POINT, SO WHAT I DON'T WANNA HEAR...

...IS A BUNCH OF P.R.-FRIENDLY SOUND BITES FROM THE GUYS AND GALS BELOW ME!

TRY COMING UP WITH SOMETHING *ACTUALLY HEROIC* TO SAY!

...BUT NOW I'VE GOT NO CLUE WHAT THIS GUY'S THINKING...

CHATTER

IT LOOKED LIKE HE WAS BEING GROUCHY A SECOND AGO...

A HERO WHO BROKE INTO THE TOP THREE DURING THE LAST RANKING.

HE STARTED HIS OWN AGENCY AT JUST 18...

...AND MADE IT INTO THE TOP TEN OF THAT YEAR'S SECOND RANKING.

HAWKS, AGE 22.

THE WORLD'S FIRST EVER TO MAKE TOP TEN AS A TEEN-AGER.

PEOPLE SAY HE DOES THINGS A LITTLE TOO FAST!

THAT FAST, THAT YOUNG!!

CHATTER

CHATTER

ARROGANT JERK.

TALK ABOUT DOING THINGS AT YER OWN PACE...

THAT'S ALL FROM ME.

DUDE WITH A LOWER APPROVAL RATING THAN ME...

MR. NUMBER ONE.

YOU'RE NEXT.

FHOOSH

SHP

FWIP

IT'S HARD TO ARGUE AGAINST WHAT HAWKS SAID.

HE'S A TOUGH ACT FOR ENDEAVOR TO FOLLOW...

AFTER MY JUNIOR COLLEAGUE FANNED THE FLAMES LIKE THAT...

SH

P

I DON'T HAVE MUCH TO SAY.

WHAT PURPOSE DOES OUR STRENGTH SERVE?

THE ANSWER IS A SIMPLE ONE.

SO, #1 HERO...

WHAT'S IT MEAN TO BE THE SYMBOL OF PEACE?

EXCEPT... JUST WATCH ME!

CLAP

CLAP

ENDEAVOR

EXPLAIN YOURSELF, KID!

GWOOOM

YIKES! SORRY FOR PUTTING YOU ON THE SPOT THERE!

NO WAY! MORE LIKE ASSISTING!

SHUP

IT DID THE TRICK, RIGHT?

TESTING ME, HUH?

Hot, hot.

SHZZ

SHZZ

...THOUGHT WE NEEDED TO SHAKE THINGS UP.

EVERYONE WAS JUST RATTLING OFF THE USUAL LINES, SO I...

BUT EVEN SO, HIM STEPPING DOWN CAME AS A SHOCK TO ME.

I NEVER WANTED TO BE LIKE HIM.

I WASN'T A BIG FAN OF ALL MIGHT.

SO THANKS FOR THE REASSURANCE! YOU WERE COOL OUT THERE.

YOU'LL NEVER BE IDOLIZED. NOT THE WAY HE WAS.

STILL...

THERE'S NO DENYING THAT WE SERIOUSLY NEED A NEW LEADER NOW.

WE'RE DONE HERE. GO MAKE THE ROUNDS AND APOLOGIZE TO THE OTHERS.

I HATE GUYS LIKE YOU THE MOST.

I WISH I WAS LOWER DOWN. THERE'S MORE FREEDOM THERE!

Between 20th and 30th place.

DO I LOOK LIKE THE TYPE TO YOU?

HA HA HA HA!

IS THIS FOOL SERIOUS? OR MOCKING ME?

AND YOU NEVER WANTED TO TAKE ON THAT ROLE YOURSELF?

I DON'T CARE! GO AWAY!

HANG ON, I'M JUST GETTING TO THE GOOD PART!

I'M TALKING ABOUT THE NOMU. REMEMBER THEM?

BACK IN MY NECK OF THE WOODS, THERE'VE BEEN SOME NASTY SIGHTINGS.

I'M THINKING WE SHOULD TEAM UP.

I EXPECT BETTER THIS TIME.

YOUR KIND IS USUALLY CLUELESS, BUT YOU...

NO. 186 - ENDEAVOR AND HAWKS

STAFF INTRODUCTION

POCCHARI
(IKEDA-KUN)

Horikoshi's comment: What a cool character!

F-29
(FUSHIMI-KUN)

Horikoshi's comment: What a cool character!

IN CHANT MANAGER
(SAKAINO-KUN)

Horikoshi's comment: What a cool character!

PAPA RUSH
(NOGUCHI-KUN)

Horikoshi's comment: What a cool character!

HISTORY-EYE
(YUZAWA-KUN)

Horikoshi's comment: What a cool character!

YORITOMISAN
(YORITOMI-SAN)

Horikoshi's comment: What a cool character!

THREE YEARS I GAVE TO THIS COMPANY, BUT TODAY I'M TAKING IT DOWN.

MUTTER

MUTTER

MUTTER

ONCE YOU'RE GOOD AND GONE...

YOU WORTHLESS COMPANY...

BUT TODAY, MY TALE COMES TO AN END.

LIBER-ATION.

LIBER-ATION.

IT'S BEEN SUFFOCATING.

FROM AS FAR BACK AS I CAN REMEMBER, I'VE LIVED MY LIFE AS A BOOTLICKER.

META LIBERATION WAR

UNPRECEDENTED REPRINT OF DESTRO'S LIFE STORY

FLAP

LONG LIVE...

...META-HUMAN LIBER-ATION!!

TERUO HAZUKASHI (AGE 31)
QUIRK: SHAME
THE MORE EMBARRASSED HE IS,
THE STRONGER HE GETS.

SO WHAT'RE YOU IN THE MOOD TO EAT, ENDEAVOR?

WHAM WHAM

WHAM WHAM

YOU'RE HUNGRY, YEAH?

I KNOW A GREAT HOT POT PLACE WITH GOOD CHICKEN STOCK.

GAB

PRETTY BRAVE ON SUCH A COLD DAY.

WHOA, CHECK IT OUT!! WE'VE GOT A FLASHER.

FEATHERS? IT MUST BE...

KYAA

GAB

COME BACK, SCHWARTZ!!

AHH!

My little Schwartz, thank goodness.

OR A YAKITORI JOINT! THIS PLACE CALLED YORITOMI HAS AMAZING LIVER SKEWERS.

SHW-IP

SHW-IP

...

FWAH

OH, LET ME CARRY THAT UP FOR YOU, MA'AM.

HEYA.

THANK YOU.

FLOAT

HEY, IT'S HAWKS!!

YOU DON'T OFTEN SEE HIM JUST WALKING AROUND!

EXCUSE ME!

COULD MY SON HAVE YOUR AUTOGRAPH? HE'S A BIG FAN.

YO.

HAWKS, HAWKS!

ENEMIES?

WE CAUGHT THE SHOW YESTERDAY! KEEP UP THAT ARROGANT ACT AND YOU'RE GONNA MAKE MORE ENEMIES!

CONGRATS ON SECOND PLACE, HAWKS!

HIS PRESENCE... IT'S KINDA INTIMIDATING...

THAT GUY'S GOT A MEAN FACE.

THERE'S ENDEAVOR...!

CHATTER

CHATTER

HERE YOU GO, RYOSUKE. THANKS FOR BEING A FAN.

RYOSUKE!

WHAT'S YOUR NAME, KID?

OF COURSE!

ON A SWELL BACKPACK LIKE THIS? SURE YOU WANT ME WRITING ON IT?

TOUCH TOUCH

YAY

I DO! BUT IT'D JUST BE WRONG!!

BUT YOU SAID YOU LIKED HIM!

NO WAY.

HEY. GO GET HIS AUTOGRAPH.

CRAP CRAP CRAP! THAT NEW COSTUME'S JUST TOO COOL!

WHA-?! WHA-?! WHY?!

HE'S COMING THIS WAY!

ACK!

THR

UST

DON'T LET ME SCARE YOU OFF NOW.

WRONG? HOW?!

THIS IS WRONG.

THIS IS WRONG?

It worked just fine with that buzz-cut guy from Shiketsu...

ENDEAVOR'S CHANGED!! FOR THE WORSE!!

WAAAH

THE ENDEAVOR I KNOW DOESN'T DO THIS KINDA STUFF FOR FANS!! HE'S TOO COOL TO STOOP TO THAT LEVEL!

SO SERIOUS ABOUT IT.

SHAKA

FAN SERVICE

HA HA HA HA!

15F YAKITORI YORITOMI MIDORI
14F SEAFOOD PALACE
13F FUKUICHI HOT POT
12F OYSTER BAR   IZAKAYA RAKUZA
11F IROHA JAPANESE DINING
10F

20F
19F
18F
17F
16F

YOU GLUTTON.

Go on. Eat your fill.

OH. ARE YOU GONNA FINISH THAT?

IT'S JUST NOT IN YOUR CHARACTER.

THAT'S WHAT THEY'LL TELL YOU, YEAH...

MUNCH MUNCH MUNCH

LIKE AFTER THE SPORTS FESTIVAL, WHEN I TRIED SCOUTING YOUR BOY.

THE SON OF NUMBER TWO WOULD'VE BEEN A NICE FEATHER IN MY CAP.

A good attention grabber.

THAT'S HOW I AM. WHEN I WANT SOMETHING, I GO FOR IT.

YOU'RE NO U.A. ALUM, BUT YOU SURE STAY INFORMED.

SINCE LITTLE SHOTO TARNISHED HIS REP BY FAILING HIS LICENSING EXAM.

BUT NOW I'M GLAD IT WAS TSUKUYOMI WHO CAME TO ME.

*TSUKUYOMI IS TOKOYAMI'S HERO NAME!

WHY'D YOU REALLY DRAG ME DOWN TO KYUSHU?

CUT THE CRAP.

I KEEP MY EYES AND EARS OPEN.

FWIP FWIP

THE *RUMORS?*

GET TO THE POINT ALREADY.

THE LEAGUE'S FREAKY REMODELED PUPPETS.

THOSE NOMU...

THE LEAGUE'S MADE SOME TROUBLE SINCE THEN, BUT THERE HAVEN'T BEEN ANY MORE NOMU SIGHTINGS.

WHEN WE CAPTURED ALL FOR ONE, WE ALSO FOUND A FEW DOZEN THAT WERE STASHED AWAY IN KAMINO.

SO YOU MUST HAVE PROOF IF YOU'RE SUGGESTING TEAMING UP...

YOU'RE THE ONE TALKING *RUMORS.*

THOSE ARE THE TWO LINES OF THOUGHT.

...OR THERE'S MORE, BUT ONLY OLD A.F.O. KNOWS WHERE THEY ARE.

SO EITHER YOU ROUNDED UP ALL OF THEM...

THE NOMU SIGHTINGS AREN'T JUST HAPPENING *HERE.*

HOLD ON, NOW. LISTEN.

OR HAVEN'T YOU HEARD?

CHECK! I'M OUT OF HERE!

FLARE

NOPE, NO PROOF. JUST RUMORS.

...ENOUGH THAT HOUSEWIVES...

... BUT...

...AND SCHOOLKIDS ARE GOSSIPING ABOUT IT.

THESE STORIES ARE SPRINGING UP ALL OVER THE COUNTRY.

WELL, NOT ENOUGH TO MAKE IT INTO THE PAPERS...

SO I TEAMED UP WITH THE POLICE, THOUGH WE KEPT THE INVESTIGATION UNDER WRAPS TO AVOID PANIC. NOTHING TURNED UP.

I FIRST HEARD ABOUT IT FROM THE LOCALS WHEN I WAS AWAY ON BUSINESS.

MEANING?

INQUIRIES...?

THERE ARE SLIGHT DISCREPANCIES BETWEEN ACCOUNTS, BUT SIMILAR STORIES ARE POPPING UP IN UNRELATED AREAS.

STILL, TOTALLY UNSUBSTANTIATED AT THIS POINT.

FW AP

STILL...

I WAS CURIOUS.

SO I'VE BEEN FLYING AROUND THE COUNTRY MAKING SOME INQUIRIES OF MY OWN.

THOSE **REMODELED** VILLAINS ARE JUST ABOUT THE CREEPIEST THINGS ON PEOPLE'S MINDS, RIGHT?

AFTER U.A., HOSU CITY AND KAMINO...

NOW, I'M TALKING PURELY HYPOTHETICAL, BUT...

AND NOW THOSE TALES ARE SPREADING ACROSS THE COUNTRY.

BUT I SAY SOME IDIOT GOT IT IN THEIR HEAD TO TELL A FEW TALES AND RILE PEOPLE UP.

THEY REPUBLISHED SOME OLD-SCHOOL CRIMINAL'S AUTOBIOGRAPHY, AND IT'S FLYING OFF THE SHELVES.

I'M THINKING THAT'S INFLUENCING PEOPLE.

THIS IS KINDA LIKE THAT.

THAT GUY EARLIER, SCREAMING "LONG LIVE METAHUMAN LIBERATION"...

WHAT'RE YOU GETTING AT, HERE? SPIT IT OUT.

GRR GRR

WELL AIN'T YOU A KNOW-IT-ALL.

THAT STUFF TENDS TO SELL BEST WHEN SOCIETY'S FEELING UNSTABLE, RIGHT?

PUFF OUT YOUR CHEST AND GIVE THEM THE MESSAGE!

WHILE I SIT BACK AND TAKE IT EASY!

I WANT OUR TOP HERO TO BE A LEADER WE CAN RELY ON!

...AND TELL EVERY-ONE THERE'S NOTHING TO FEAR!

YOU SHOULD BE THE ONE TO LOOK INTO THESE OMINOUS RUMORS...

DO SOME LEISURELY PATROLLING, PUT IN A FEW APPEARANCES...

SERIOUSLY.

I JUST WANNA ENJOY MYSELF.

...SAY "AW SHUCKS, NO TROUBLE TODAY" AND GET A GOOD NIGHT'S SLEEP! THAT'S MY IDEAL LIFE!

THIS IS YOUR SHOW TO DIRECT, MR. NUMBER ONE.

LIKE I BASICALLY SAID YESTERDAY...

WHAT KINDA STANCE IS THAT?

YOUR BILL, GENTLE-MEN.

...

GET BACK, MISS!

FWOO

YOU WANT NUMBER ONE? YOU GOT HIM!

C'MON!

FLASH-FIRE FIST...

STREET CLOTHES

Birthday: 3/1
Height: 159 cm
Favorite Thing: Carrots

THE SUPPLEMENT
Designwise, she's an amalgamation of my likes and preferences.

Her hero name is a reference to a certain MMA fighter.

THANKS, AS ALWAYS!

I'LL LEAVE YOUR CLEAN LAUNDRY OVER HERE, MOM.

NO. 187 - FLAMING ROAR! VS. NOMU: HIGH-END

NATSUO TODOROKI (19) SHOTO'S BROTHER

WE DON'T DO SO WELL WITH HEAT.

GOOD. I LIKE THE COLD, YOU KNOW.

FUYUMI TODOROKI (22) SHOTO'S SISTER

IT'S SUPPOSED TO GET REALLY COLD NEXT WEEK.

YOU'RE LOOKING WELL, NATSU.

REI TODOROKI SHOTO'S MOTHER

LOOKS NICE AND HEALTHY!!

YOUR COMPLEXION...

A-ANYWAY, YOU'RE LOOKING GOOD TOO, MOM!

I CALL HOME NOW AND THEN. AIN'T THAT ENOUGH?!

SIS!!

DID YOU FIND YOURSELF A GIRLFRIEND IN ONE OF YOUR SEMINARS?

WE DON'T SEE YOU MUCH, EVER SINCE YOU STARTED COLLEGE.

Yikes!

HE'S STRUGGLING WITH THE EXTRA LICENSE TRAINING...

...BUT HE'S WORKING HARD TO KEEP UP WITH HIS FRIENDS.

FWIP

YES, SHOTO'S BEEN SENDING ME LETTERS.

I SUPPOSE THAT'S UP TO MY DOCTOR...

Writing actual letters is rough.

CAN'T THEY JUST LET YOU HAVE A CELL PHONE ALREADY?

SHWIP

BECAUSE OF TRAINING AND THE DORM SYSTEM, HE CAN'T STOP BY AS MUCH ANYMORE.

I DIDN'T THINK SHOTO WAS THE TYPE TO WRITE HOME.

OH?

FWIP

MOM.

THEY MADE HIM NUMBER ONE YESTERDAY. IT'S OFFICIAL.

ABOUT HIM...

THE WORLD STILL DOESN'T KNOW THE TRUTH ABOUT YOU. ABOUT OUR SIBLINGS...

ABOUT HOW HE'S ALWAYS TREATED HIS FAMILY.

FOR ONE, HE DOESN'T DO THE TALK SHOW CIRCUIT.

NATSU.

THINKING BACK, HE WAS LIKE A PERFECT STRANGER.

I CAN BARELY REMEMBER MOST OF IT, REALLY.

WHY'D YOU HAVE TO BRING UP DAD?

IT'S FINE, FUYUMI.

WHAT HE DID TO YOU, TO SHOTO AND TO... WELL, I CAN'T LET ANYONE PRETEND IT ALL NEVER HAPPENED...

BUT...

IT'S LIKE HE WANTS TO LEAVE IT ALL BEHIND.

HIS PAST, HIS FAMILY...

AND HE STILL HASN'T COME TO APOLOGIZE TO YOU.

IT'S BEEN ALMOST TEN YEARS.

WHY'RE YOU DEFENDING HIM? C'MON, MOM.

THAT'S...

...NOT TRUE.

I TOLD HIM THEY WERE MY FAVORITE.

THOSE FLOWERS...

?

DAD REALLY SHOWED UP HERE?!

AND MY DOCTOR SAYS IT'S NOT A GOOD IDEA.

APPARENTLY, HE'S COME MANY TIMES.

THOUGH...WE HAVEN'T MET. I'M A BIT SCARED THOUGH...

BACK WHEN WE FIRST MET, I TOLD HIM.

ONLY ONCE.

HE'S NOT LEAVING ANYTHING BEHIND.

BUT...

IT MIGHT BE EXTERNAL PRESSURES.

OF COURSE, I CAN'T SAY WHAT HE'S THINKING.

JUST WATCH ME!

NOT HIS PAST. NOT HIS FAMILY.

I KNOW HE'S TRYING TO MAKE SENSE OF IT ALL!

NO. 187 - FLAMING ROAR! VS. NOMU: HIGH-END

WHOOOOOOSH

STAY ALERT! THIS GUY'S...

...JUST GETTING STARTED!

I'M NOT FLYING. MORE LIKE NOT FALLING.

I DIDN'T KNOW YOU COULD FLY, ENDEAVOR!!

...THAT FIRE COULD...

...KILL...

...KILL-KILL...

SZZZ

YOU-YOU REALLY THOUGHT...

RIGHT... IT POSSESSES STRONG QUIRKS...

REGENER-ATING, HUH?

...ME?

SHK

LURP

PLUS...

MAKING THIS ONE SOME-THING REAL SPECIAL, EVEN COMPARED TO THOSE OTHERS.

MEANING, THE BLACK NOMU ARE IN A LEAGUE OF THEIR OWN...

THEN THERE WAS ANOTHER ONE IN HOSU...

THEY SAY THE NOMU THAT HIT U.A. WERE LIKE THIS...

BUT THE WHITE ONES WERE DIFFERENT.

STREET CLOTHES

Birthday: 12/28
Height: 172 cm
Favorite Thing: Chicken [as food]

DEEP BEHIND THE SCENES

He was originally going to be a man with a bird head. Basically, the reappropriated design of Takahiro, from one of my older series. I'll be honest—I love bird people. You can blame *Mashin Hero Wataru* for that.

So how'd he get this human head? Well, during production of the movie, the anime staff came to me and asked, "Can we use Takahiro?" It was deeply moving to think that they had read my earlier series and wanted to show it some love. My life is basically peaking with this movie, so of course I agreed with enthusiasm. Not a big deal to change Hawks' design, after all.

After that, my staff had a lukewarm reaction to the idea of a birdman being number two, but I settled on this safe and sound (?) design for the guy.

BURN IT TO BITS!!

SHK
SHK
SHK

NO. 188 - YOUR FATHER, THE NUMBER ONE HERO

IN AN INSTANT...

THAT'S GODLIKE!

HE'S CUTTING IT APART WITH FIRE!

WHOOSH

SW SIS 44

FWAH FWAH

Roll Roll Roll

HAVEN'T...

...YOU...

...EVER COOKED ANYTHING, ENDEAVOR?

QUIT YAPPING AND TIGHTEN UP YOUR SLOPPY MOVES.

WHEN CHOPPING, YOU GOTTA MAKE THE PIECES UNIFORM.

Ouch!

YEAH, BUT WHEN I SEND OUT TOO MANY FEATHERS, MY FLYING TAKES A HIT.

WELL, EXCUSE ME!

THUD

THUD

BOOM

!

BIRD...

SWIP

SWIP

ENDEAVOR! HAWKS!! WE GOT YOUR BACKS!!

F-WUMP

F-WUMP

BWOOM

...INTER-INTERFERE.

BOOM

D-DON'T...

BOOM

- *FLIES VIA **SHOULDER-MOUNTED JETS***

- ***TRANSFORMING ARMS** AID IN FLIGHT BUT CAN ALSO STRETCH AND SPLIT APART*

- *STRETCHED-OUT ARMS ARE STRENGTHENED BY **MUSCULAR ENHANCEMENT***

- *ENOUGH **POWER** TO SMASH STRAIGHT THROUGH REINFORCED CONCRETE*

- *PLUS **REGENERATION***

THAT MAKES FIVE!

AND THE SIXTH...

FISSION!

THEY'RE A DIFFERENT COLOR, THOUGH... SO MAYBE THEY'RE JUST STORED IN ITS BODY?

SO TO KEEP THE FIGHT WITH ME GOING, IT'S DIVERTING OUR BACKUP.

I'M REALLY STARTING TO OVERHEAT...

TAKING THIS THING AT FACE VALUE, IT'S OUT TO FIGHT SOMEONE STRONG. THAT'S PRETTY COMMON THINKING FOR VILLAINS!

...INTERFERED.

FUN-FUN...

WHO'S THE BEST HERE?

TWIST

BOOM

B

...THINKING!

THIS NOMU IS...

WORMP

WORMP

Grah!

WAAAH! GET AWAY!!

SLASH!!

AND I AIN'T GUARANTEEING ANYTHING, ESPECIALLY WHEN IT'S MY OWN NECK ON THE LINE...

FWAH

HAWKS!

WHOA!

YEP, IT'S ME.

NOW LET'S GET YOU GUYS SOMEWHERE NICE AND FAR AWAY.

BECAUSE IN ALL HONESTY, I CAN'T DO MUCH AGAINST BRUTE STRENGTH.

IT POSSES- SES GOOD INTUITION, TOO.

OR-OR, CAN'T SHOOT MORE...? IN THAT- THAT CASE...

...

WHOOSH

NOT... SHOOT- SHOOTING... ANYMORE...

H-HEAT AND FIRE-FIRE LINES?

MY FLASHFIRE FIST CONDENSES MY FLAMES TO WHITE-HOT POINTS. IT'S SUPPOSED TO BE MY ONE-HIT FINISHER.

RAMPANT USE RAISES MY BODY HEAT, WHICH SLOWS DOWN MY WHOLE SYSTEM...

I'M ALREADY AT A DISADVANTAGE IN BOTH SPEED AND POWER. I DON'T KNOW HOW MANY QUIRKS IT'S ACTUALLY GOT, EITHER. HOLDING BACK COULD PROVE DEADLY!

FSSH

MY BODY JUST KEEPS OVERHEATING...

AND...

...YOU...

AND YOU GUYS...

THAT'S WHY... WITH YOU...

I'M GOING TO TODOROKI.

KLICK

GUYS...

KEEP AN EYE ON ERI.

FWIP

LET'S TAKE A TRIP BACK TO YOUR ROOM, ERI.

OKAY.

ENDEAVOR ...!!

VOLUME 20 - SCHOOL FESTIVAL START!! (END)

MY HERO ACADEMIA

reads from right to left, starting in the upper-right corner. Japanese is read from right to left, meaning that action, sound effects and word-balloon order are completely reversed from English order.